30232953R00086

Printed in Great
Britain
by Amazon